Introduction

I can think of no greater privilege then to publish all 10 of Neville Goddard's spiritual classics in this convenient pocket book format.

These 4.5 x 7" paperbacks are perfect for those times that your "Neville Goddard: The Complete Reader" is just a little too big to bring on your day out. Fit them in your pocket or purse and take your favorite metaphysical classic to keep you company. As an added bonus, all 10 classics are now available on iTunes as audio books for those that prefer the spoken word.

Check our website often as our selection of pocket books grows and continues to give you a wide range of truths and wisdom from the most sacred wisdom traditions available. We love "Giving Voice to the Wisdom of the Ages", and hope you enjoy the effort.

Barry J Peterson

MetaPhysicalPocketBooks.Com
AudioEnlightenment.Com

AWAKENED IMAGINATION & THE SEARCH

Neville Goddard

Compiled & Edited
Barry J Peterson

Published by Metaphysicalpocketbooks.com

Giving Voice to the Wisdom of the Ages

Printed in the United States of America

0 1 2 3 4 5 6 7 8 9

First Printing, 2017

ISBN 978-1-941489-22-2

www.MetaphysicalPocketBooks.Com
www.AudioEnlightenment.Com

Awakened Imagination & the Search, and the entire 10 Book Series by Neville Goddard Is now available in iTunes as a downloadable Audio Book

First "Metaphysicalpocketbooks.com" Printing August, 2017

Contents

WHO IS YOUR IMAGINATION?

> I rest not from my great task to open
> the Eternal Worlds, to open the
> immortal Eyes of Man inwards into the
> Worlds of thought: into Eternity ever
> expanding in the Bosom of God,
> the Human Imagination.
> . . . Blake, Jerusalem 5:18-20

CERTAIN WORDS in the course of long use gather so many strange connotations that they almost cease to mean anything at all. Such a word is imagination. This word is made to serve all manner of ideas, some of them directly opposed to one another. Fancy, thought, hallucination, suspicion: indeed, so wide is its use and so varied its meanings, the word imagination has no status nor fixed significance.

For example, we ask a man to "use his imagination", meaning that his present outlook is too restricted and therefore not equal to the task. In the next breath, we tell him that his ideas are "pure imagination", thereby implying that his ideas are unsound. We speak of a jealous or suspicious person as a "victim of his own imagination", meaning that his thoughts are untrue. A minute later we pay a man the highest tribute by describing him as a "man of imagination".

Thus the word imagination has no definite meaning. Even the dictionary gives us no help. It defines imagination as (1) the picturing power or act of the mind, the constructive or creative principle; (2) a phantasm; (3) an irrational notion or belief; (4) planning, plotting or scheming as involving mental construction.

I identify the central figure of the Gospels with human imagination, the power which makes the forgiveness of sins, the achievement of our goals, inevitable.

All things were made by Him; and without
Him was not anything made that was made.
. . . John 1:3

There is only one thing in the world, Imagination, and all our deformations of it.

WHO IS YOUR IMAGINATION?

He is despised and rejected of men; a man of
sorrows, and acquainted with grief.
. . . Isaiah 53:3

Imagination is the very gateway of reality.

"Man", said Blake, "is either the ark of God or
a phantom of the earth and of the water".
"Naturally he is only a natural organ subject to
Sense". "The Eternal Body of Man is The
Imagination: that is God himself, The Divine
Body.   [yod, shin, ayin; from right to the left]:
Jesus: we are His Members".

I know of no greater and truer definition of the
Imagination than that of Blake. By imagination we
have the power to be anything we desire to be.

Through imagination, we disarm and
transform the violence of the world. Our most
intimate as well as our most casual relationships
become imaginative, as we awaken to "the mystery
hid from the ages", that Christ in us is our
imagination. We then realize that only as we live
by imagination can we truly be said to live at all.

I want this book to be the simplest, clearest,
frankest work I have the power to make it, that I

may encourage you to function imaginatively, that you may open your "Immortal Eyes inwards into the Worlds of Thought", where you behold every desire of your heart as ripe grain "white already to harvest".

> I am come that they might have life,
> and that they might have it more abundantly.
> . . . John 10:10

The abundant life that Christ promised us is ours to experience now, but not until we have the sense of Christ as our imagination can we experience it.

> The mystery hid from the ages...
> Christ in you, the hope of glory,
> . . . Colossians 1:26, 27

is your imagination. This is the mystery which I am ever striving to realize more keenly myself and to urge upon others.

Imagination is our redeemer, "the Lord from Heaven" born of man but not begotten of man.

Every man is Mary and birth to Christ must give. If the story of the Immaculate Conception and birth of Christ appears irrational to man, it is only because it is misread as biography, history, and cosmology, and the modern explorers of the imagination do not help by calling It the unconscious or subconscious mind. Imagination's birth and growth is the gradual transition from a God of tradition to a God of experience. If the birth of Christ in man seems slow, it is only because man is unwilling to let go the comfortable but false anchorage of tradition.

When imagination is discovered as the first principle of religion, the stone of literal understanding will have felt the rod of Moses and, like the rock of Zin, issue forth the water of psychological meaning to quench the thirst of humanity; and all who take the proffered cup and live a life according to this truth will transform the water of psychological meaning into the wine of forgiveness. Then, like the good Samaritan, they will pour it on the wounds of all.

The Son of God is not to be found in history, nor in any external form. He can only be found as the imagination of him in whom His presence becomes manifest.

WHO IS YOUR IMAGINATION?

O, would thy heart but be a manger for His
birth! God would once more become a child
on earth.

Man is the garden in which this only-begotten
Son of God sleeps. He awakens this Son by lifting
his imagination up to heaven and clothing men in
godlike stature. We must go on imagining better
than the best we know.

Man in the moment of his awakening to the
imaginative life must meet the test of Sonship.

"Father, reveal Thy Son in me" and
"It pleased God to reveal His Son in me".
. . . Galatians 1:15, 16

The supreme test of Sonship is the forgiveness
of sin. The test that your imagination is Christ
Jesus, the Son of God, is your ability to forgive
sin. Sin means missing one's mark in life, falling
short of one's ideal, failing to achieve one's aim.
Forgiveness means identification of man with his
ideal or aim in life. This is the work of awakened
imagination, the supreme work, for it tests man's
ability to enter into and partake of the nature of his
opposite.

WHO IS YOUR IMAGINATION?

Let the weak man say, I am strong.
... Joel 3:10

Reasonably, this is impossible. Only awakened imagination can enter into and partake of the nature of its opposite.

This conception of Christ Jesus as human imagination raises these fundamental questions: Is imagination a power sufficient, not merely to enable me to assume that I am strong, but is it also of itself capable of executing the idea? Suppose that I desire to be in some other place or situation. Could I, by imagining myself into such a state and place, bring about their physical realization? Suppose I could not afford the journey and suppose my present social and financial status oppose the idea that I want to realize. Would imagination be sufficient of itself to incarnate these desires? Does imagination comprehend reason? By reason, I mean deductions from the observations of the senses.

Does it recognize the external world of facts? In the practical way of everyday life is imagination a complete guide to behavior? Suppose I am capable of acting with continuous imagination, that is, suppose I am capable of sustaining the feeling of my wish fulfilled, will my assumption harden into fact?

And, if it does harden into fact, shall I on reflection find that my actions through the period of incubation have been reasonable? Is my imagination a power sufficient, not merely to assume the feeling of the wish fulfilled, but is it also of itself capable of incarnating the idea? After assuming that I am already what I want to be, must I continually guide myself by reasonable ideas and actions in order to bring about the fulfillment of my assumption?

Experience has convinced me that an assumption, though false, if persisted in, will harden into fact, that continuous imagination is sufficient for all things, and all my reasonable plans and actions will never make up for my lack of continuous imagination.

Is it not true that the teachings of the Gospels can only be received in terms of faith and that the Son of God is constantly looking for signs of faith in people – that is, faith in their own imagination?

WHO IS YOUR IMAGINATION?

Is not the promise

Believe that ye receive and ye shall receive.
  . . . Mark 11:24

the same as "Imagine that you are and you shall be"? Was it not an imaginary state in which Moses

"Endured, as seeing Him who is invisible"?
  . . . Hebrews 11:27

Was it not by the power of his own imagination that he endured?

Truth depends upon the intensity of the imagination, not upon external facts. Facts are the fruit bearing witness of the use or misuse of the imagination.

Man becomes what he imagines. He has a self-determined history. Imagination is the way, the truth, the life revealed. We cannot get hold of truth with the logical mind. Where the natural man of sense sees a bud, imagination sees a rose full-blown.

Truth cannot be encompassed by facts. As we awaken to the imaginative life, we discover that to imagine a thing is to make it so, that a true judgment need not conform to the external reality to which it relates.

The imaginative man does not deny the reality of the sensuous outer world of Becoming, but he knows that it is the inner world of continuous Imagination that is the force by which the sensuous outer world of Becoming is brought to pass. He sees the outer world and all its happenings as projections of the inner world of Imagination. To him, everything is a manifestation of the mental activity which goes on in man's imagination, without the sensuous reasonable man being aware of it. But he realizes that every man must become conscious of this inner activity and see the relationship between the inner causal world of imagination and the sensuous outer world of effects.

It is a marvelous thing to find that you can imagine yourself into the state of your fulfilled desire and escape from the jails which ignorance built.

The Real Man is a Magnificent Imagination. It is this self that must be awakened.

WHO IS YOUR IMAGINATION?

Awake thou that sleepest, and arise from the
dead, and Christ shall give thee light.
. . . Ephesians 5:14

The moment man discovers that his
imagination is Christ, he accomplishes acts which
on this level can only be called miraculous. But
until man has the sense of Christ as his
imagination,

"You did not choose me,
I have chosen you."
. . . John 15:16

He will see everything in pure objectivity
without any subjective relationship. Not realizing
that all that he encounters is part of himself, he
rebels at the thought that he has chosen the
conditions of his life, that they are related by
affinity to his own mental activity. Man must
firmly come to believe that reality lies within him
and not without.

Although others have bodies, a life of their
own, their reality is rooted in you, ends in you, as
yours ends in God.

SEALED INSTRUCTIONS

The first power that meets us at the
threshold of the soul's domain is the power
of imagination.
. . . Dr. Franz Hartmann

I WAS FIRST made conscious of the power, nature, and redemptive function of imagination through the teachings of my friend Abdullah; and through subsequent experiences, I learned that Jesus was a symbol of the coming of imagination to man, that the test of His birth in man was the individual's ability to forgive sin; that is, his ability to identify himself or another with his aim in life.

Without the identification of man with his aim, the forgiveness of sin is an impossibility, and only the Son of God can forgive sin. Therefore, man's ability to identify himself with his aim, though reason and his senses deny it, is proof of the birth of Christ in him. To passively surrender to appearances and bow before the evidence of facts is to confess that Christ is not yet born in you.

SEALED INSTRUCTIONS

Although this teaching shocked and repelled me at first – for I was a convinced and earnest Christian, and did not then know that Christianity could not be inherited by the mere accident of birth but must be consciously adopted as a way of life – it stole later on, through visions, mystical revelations, and practical experiences, into my understanding and found its interpretation in a deeper mood. But I must confess that it is a trying time when those things are shaken which one has always taken for granted.

> Seest thou these great buildings? There shall
> not be left one stone upon another that shall
> not be thrown down.
> . . . Mark 13:2

Not one stone of literal understanding will be left after one drinks the water of psychological meaning.

All that has been built up by natural religion is cast into the flames of mental fire. Yet, what better way is there to understand Christ Jesus than to identify the central character of the Gospels with human imagination – knowing that, every time you exercise your imagination lovingly on behalf of another, you are literally mediating God to man and thereby feeding and clothing Christ Jesus and that, whenever you imagine evil against another, you are literally beating and crucifying Christ Jesus?

Every imagination of man is either the cup of cold water or the sponge of vinegar to the parched lips of Christ.

Let none of you imagine evil in your hearts against his neighbor warned the prophet Zechariah.

When man heeds this advice, he will awake from the imposed sleep of Adam into the full consciousness of the Son of God. He is in the world, and the world is made by Him, and the world knows Him not: Human Imagination.

I asked myself many times, "If my imagination is Christ Jesus and all things are possible to Christ Jesus, are all things possible to me?"

Through experience, I have come to know that, when I identify myself with my aim in life, then Christ is awake in me. Christ is sufficient for all things.

21

SEALED INSTRUCTIONS

I lay down My life that I might take it again.
No man taketh it from Me, but I lay it down
of Myself.
. . . John 10:17, 18

What a comfort it is to know that all that I experience is the result of my own standard of beliefs; that I am the center of my own web of circumstances and that as I change, so must my outer world!

The world presents different appearances according as our states of consciousness differ. What we see when we are identified with a state cannot be seen when we are no longer fused with it. By state is meant all that man believes and consents to as true. No idea presented to the mind can realize itself unless the mind accepts it. It depends on the acceptance, the state with which we are identified, how things present themselves. In the fusion of imagination and states is to be found the shaping of the world as it seems. The world is a revelation of the states with which imagination is fused. It is the state from which we think that determines the objective world in which we live. The rich man, the poor man, the good man, the thief are what they are by virtue of the states from which they view the world. On the distinction between these states depends the distinction between the worlds of these men. Individually so different is this same world. It is not the actions and behavior of the good man that should be matched but his point of view.

Outer reforms are useless if the inner state is not changed. Success is gained not by imitating the outer actions of the successful but by right inner actions and inner talking.

If we detach ourselves from a state, and we may at any moment, the conditions and circumstances to which that union gave being vanish.

It was in the fall of 1933 in New York City that I approached Abdullah with a problem. He asked me one simple question, "What do you want?"

I told him that I would like to spend the winter in Barbados, but that I was broke. I literally did not have a nickel.

"If you will imagine yourself to be in Barbados", said he, "thinking and viewing the world from that state of consciousness instead of thinking of Barbados, you will spend the winter there. You must not concern yourself with the ways and means of getting there, for the state of consciousness of already being in Barbados, if occupied by your imagination, will devise the means best suited to realize itself."

Man lives by committing himself to invisible states, by fusing his imagination with what he knows to be other than himself, and in this union he experiences the results of that fusion. No one can lose what he has, save by detachment from the state where the things experienced have their natural life.

"You must imagine yourself right into the state of your fulfilled desire", Abdullah told me, "and fall asleep viewing the world from Barbados."

The world which we describe from observation must be as we describe it relative to ourselves. Our imagination connects us with the state desired. But we must use imagination masterfully, not as an onlooker thinking of the end, but as a partaker thinking from the end. We must actually be there in imagination. If we do this, our subjective experience will be realized objectively.

SEALED INSTRUCTIONS

"This is not mere fancy", said he, "but a truth you can prove by experience."

His appeal to enter into the wish fulfilled was the secret of thinking from the end. Every state is already there as "mere possibility" as long as you think of it, but is overpoweringly real when you think from it. Thinking from the end is the way of Christ.

I began right there and then, fixing my thoughts beyond the limits of sense, beyond that aspect to which my present state gave being, towards the feeling of already being in Barbados and viewing the world from that standpoint.

He emphasized the importance of the state from which man views the world as he falls asleep. All prophets claim that the voice of God is chiefly heard by man in dreams.

In a dream, in a vision of the night, when deep sleep falleth upon men, in slumbering upon the bed; then he openeth the ears of men, and sealeth their instruction.
. . . Job 33:15, 16

SEALED INSTRUCTIONS

That night and for several nights thereafter, I fell asleep in the assumption that I was in my father's house in Barbados. Within a month, I received a letter from my brother, saying that he had a strong desire to have the family together at Christmas and asking me to use the enclosed steamship ticket for Barbados. I sailed two days after I received my brother's letter and spent a wonderful winter in Barbados.

This experience has convinced me that man can be anything he pleases if he will make the conception habitual and think from the end. It has also shown me that I can no longer excuse myself by placing the blame on the world of external things – that my good and my evil have no dependency except from myself – that it depends on the state from which I view the world how things present themselves.

Man, who is free in his choice, acts from conceptions which he freely, though not always wisely, chooses. All conceivable states are awaiting our choice and occupancy, but no amount of rationalizing will of itself yield us the state of consciousness which is the only thing worth having.

SEALED INSTRUCTIONS

The imaginative image is the only thing to seek.

The ultimate purpose of imagination is to create in us "the spirit of Jesus", which is continual forgiveness of sin, continual identification of man with his ideal. Only by identifying ourselves with our aim can we forgive ourselves for having missed it. All else is labor in vain. On this path, to whatever place or state we convey our imagination, to that place or state we will gravitate physically also.

> In My Father's house are many mansions;
> if it were not so, I would have told you.
> I go to prepare a place for you.
> And if I go and prepare a place for you,
> I will come again,
> and receive you unto Myself;
> that where I am, there ye may be also.
> . . . John 14:2, 3

By sleeping in my father's house in my imagination as though I slept there in the flesh, I fused my imagination with that state and was compelled to experience that state in the flesh also.

SEALED INSTRUCTIONS

So vivid was this state to me, I could have been seen in my father's house had any sensitive entered the room where in imagination I was sleeping. A man can be seen where in imagination he is, for a man must be where his imagination is, for his imagination is himself. This I know from experience, for I have been seen by a few to whom I desired to be seen, when physically I was hundreds of miles away.

I, by the intensity of my imagination and feeling, imagining and feeling myself to be in Barbados instead of merely thinking of Barbados, had spanned the vast Atlantic to influence my brother into desiring my presence to complete the family circle at Christmas.

Thinking from the end, from the feeling of my wish fulfilled, was the source of everything that happened as outer cause, such as my brother's impulse to send me a steamship ticket; and it was also the cause of everything that appeared as results.

In Ideas of Good and Evil, W. B. Yeats, having described a few experiences similar to this experience of mine, writes:

SEALED INSTRUCTIONS

If all who have described events like this
have not dreamed, we should rewrite our
histories, for all men, certainly all
imaginative men, must be forever casting
forth enchantments, glamour, illusions; and
all men, especially tranquil men who have
no powerful egotistic life, must be
continually passing under their power.

Determined imagination, thinking *from* the
end, is the beginning of all miracles.

I would like to give you an immense belief in
miracles, but a miracle is only the name given by
those who have no knowledge of the power and
function of imagination to the works of
imagination. Imagining oneself into the feeling of
the wish fulfilled is the means by which a new
state is entered. This gives the state the quality of
is-ness.

Hermes tells us:

That which is, is manifested; that which has
been or shall be, is unmanifested, but not
dead; for Soul, the eternal activity of God,
animates all things.

SEALED INSTRUCTIONS

The future must become the present in the imagination of the one who would wisely and consciously create circumstances. We must translate vision into Being, thinking of into thinking from. Imagination must center itself in some state and view the world from that state. Thinking from the end is an intense perception of the world of fulfilled desire. Thinking from the state desired is creative living. Ignorance of this ability to think from the end is bondage. It is the root of all bondage with which man is bound. To passively surrender to the evidence of the senses underestimates the capacities of the Inner Self. Once man accepts thinking *from* the end as a creative principle in which he can cooperate, then he is redeemed from the absurdity of ever attempting to achieve his objective by merely thinking of it.

Construct all ends according to the pattern of fulfilled desire.

The whole of life is just the appeasement of hunger, and the infinite states of consciousness from which a man can view the world are purely a means of satisfying that hunger. The principle upon which each state is organized is some form of hunger to lift the passion for self-gratification to ever higher and higher levels of experience. Desire is the mainspring of the mental machinery. It is a blessed thing. It is a right and natural craving which has a state of consciousness as its right and natural satisfaction.

> But one thing I do, forgetting the things
> which are behind, and stretching forward to
> the things which are before, I press on
> toward the goal.
> . . . Philippians 3:13, 14

It is necessary to have an aim in life. Without an aim, we drift. "What wantest thou of Me?" is the implied question asked most often by the central figure of the Gospels. In defining your aim, you must want it.

> As the hart panteth after the water brooks, so
> panteth my soul after Thee, O, God.
> . . . Psalms 42:1

It is lack of this passionate direction to life that makes man fail of accomplishment.

The spanning of the bridge between desire – thinking of – and satisfaction – thinking from is all-important. We must move mentally from thinking of the end to thinking from the end. This, reason could never do. By its nature, it is restricted to the evidence of the senses; but imagination, having no such limitation, can. Desire exists to be gratified in the activity of imagination. Through imagination, man escapes from the limitation of the senses and the bondage of reason.

There is no stopping the man who can think from the end. Nothing can stop him. He creates the means and grows his way out of limitation into ever greater and greater mansions of the Lord. It does not matter what he has been or what he is. All that matters is "what does he want?"

He knows that the world is a manifestation of the mental activity which goes on within himself, so he strives to determine and control the ends from which he thinks. In his imagination he dwells in the end, confident that he shall dwell there in the flesh also. He puts his whole trust in the feeling of the wish fulfilled and lives by committing himself to that state, for the art of fortune is to tempt him so to do. Like the man at the pool of Bethesda, he is ready for the moving of the waters of imagination. Knowing that every desire is ripe grain to him who knows how to think from the end, he is indifferent to mere reasonable probability and confident that through continuous imagination his assumptions will harden into fact.

But how to persuade men everywhere that thinking from the end is the only living, how to foster it in every activity of man, how to reveal it as the plenitude of life and not the compensation of the disappointed: that is the problem.

Life is a controllable thing. You can experience what you please once you realize that you are His Son, and that you are what you are by virtue of the state of consciousness from which you think and view the world,

Son, Thou art ever with Me,
and all that I have is Thine.
. . . Luke 15:31

HIGHWAYS OF THE INNER WORLD

And the children struggled within her... and
the Lord said unto her, two nations are in thy
womb, and two manner of people shall be
separated from thy bowels; and the one
people shall be stronger than the other
people; and the elder shall serve the
younger.
. . . Genesis 25:22,23

DUALITY IS an inherent condition of life.
Everything that exists is double. Man is a dual
creature with contrary principles embedded in his
nature. They war within him and present attitudes
to life which are antagonistic. This conflict is the
eternal enterprise, the war in heaven, the never-
ending struggle of the younger or inner man of
imagination to assert His supremacy over the elder
or outer man of sense.

The first shall be last and the last shall be
first.
. . . Matthew 19:30

He it is, Who coming after me is preferred
before me.
. . . John 1:27

The second Man is the Lord from heaven.
. . . 1Corinthians 15:47

Man begins to awake to the imaginative life
the moment he feels the presence of another being
in himself.

In your limbs lie nations twain, rival races
from their birth; one the mastery shall gain,
the younger o'er the elder reign.

There are two distinct centers of thought or
outlooks on the world possessed by every man.
The Bible speaks of these two outlooks as natural
and spiritual.

The natural man receiveth not the things of
the Spirit of God: for they are foolishness
unto him: neither can he know them,
because they are spiritually discerned.
. . . 1Corinthians 2:14

Man's inner body is as real in the world of
subjective experience as his outer physical body is

real in the world of external realities, but the inner body expresses a more fundamental part of reality. This existing inner body of man must be consciously exercised and directed. The inner world of thought and feeling to which the inner body is attuned has its real structure and exists in its own higher space.

There are two kinds of movement, one that is according to the inner body and another that is according to the outer body. The movement which is according to the inner body is causal, but the outer movement is under compulsion. The inner movement determines the outer which is joined to it, bringing into the outer a movement that is similar to the actions of the inner body. Inner movement is the force by which all events are brought to pass. Outer movement is subject to the compulsion applied to it by the movement of the inner body.

Whenever the actions of the inner body match the actions which the outer must take to appease desire, that desire will be realized.

Construct mentally a drama which implies that your desire is realized and make it one which involves movement of self. Immobilize your outer physical self. Act precisely as though you were going to take a nap, and start the predetermined action in imagination.

A vivid representation of the action is the beginning of that action. Then, as you are falling asleep, consciously imagine yourself into the scene. The length of the sleep is not important, a short nap is sufficient, but carrying the action into sleep thickens fancy into fact.

At first your thoughts may be like rambling sheep that have no shepherd. Don't despair. Should your attention stray seventy times seven, bring it back seventy times seven to its predetermined course until from sheer exhaustion it follows the appointed path. The inner journey must never be without direction. When you take to the inner road, it is to do what you did mentally before you started. You go for the prize you have already seen and accepted.

In The Road to *Xanadu*, Professor John Livingston Lowes says:

But I have long had the feeling, which this study had matured to a conviction, that Fancy and Imagination are not two powers at all, but one. The valid distinction which exists between them lies, not in the materials with which they operate, but in the degree of intensity of the operant power itself. Working at high tension, the imaginative energy assimilates and transmutes; keyed low, the same energy aggregates and yokes together those images which at its highest pitch, it merges indissolubly into one.

Fancy assembles, imagination fuses.

Here is a practical application of this theory. A year ago, a blind girl living in the city of San Francisco found herself confronted with a transportation problem. A rerouting of buses forced her to make three transfers between her home and her office. This lengthened her trip from fifteen minutes to two hours and fifteen minutes. She thought seriously about this problem and came to the decision that a car was the solution. She knew that she could not drive a car but felt that she could be driven in one. Putting this theory to the test that "whenever the actions of the inner self correspond to the actions which the outer, physical self must take to appease desire, that desire will be realized", she said to herself, "I will sit here and imagine that I am being driven to my office."

Sitting in her living room, she began to imagine herself seated in a car. She felt the rhythm of the motor. She imagined that she smelled the odor of gasoline, felt the motion of the car, touched the sleeve of the driver and felt that the driver was a man. She felt the car stop, and turning to her companion, said, "Thank you very much, sir."

To which he replied, "The pleasure is all mine."

Then she stepped from the car and heard the door snap shut as she closed it.

She told me that she centered her imagination on being in a car and, although blind, viewed the city from her imaginary ride. She did not think of the ride. She thought from the ride and all that it implied. This controlled and subjectively directed purposive ride raised her imagination to its full potency. She kept her purpose ever before her, knowing there was cohesion in purposive inner movement. In these mental journeys an emotional continuity must be sustained – the emotion of fulfilled desire. Expectancy and desire were so intensely joined that they passed at once from a mental state into a physical act.

HIGHWAYS OF THE INNER WORLD

The inner self moves along the predetermined course best when the emotions collaborate. The inner self must be fired, and it is best fired by the thought of great deeds and personal gain. We must take pleasure in our actions.

On two successive days, the blind girl took her imaginary ride, giving it all the joy and sensory vividness of reality. A few hours after her second imaginary ride, a friend told her of a story in the evening paper. It was a story of a man who was interested in the blind. The blind girl phoned him and stated her problem. The very next day, on his way home, he stopped in at a bar and while there had the urge to tell the story of the blind girl to his friend the proprietor. A total stranger, on hearing the story, volunteered to drive the blind girl home every day. The man who told the story then said, "If you will take her home, I will take her to work."

This was over a year ago, and since that day, this blind girl has been driven to and from her office by these two gentlemen. Now, instead of spending two hours and fifteen minutes on three buses, she is at her office in less than fifteen minutes. And on that first ride to her office, she turned to her good Samaritan and said, "Thank you very much, sir"; and he replied, "The pleasure is all mine."

Thus, the objects of her imagination were to her the realities of which the physical manifestation was only the witness. The determinative animating principle was the imaginative ride. Her triumph could be a surprise only to those who did not know of her inner ride. She mentally viewed the world from this imaginative ride with such a clearness of vision that every aspect of the city attained identity.

These inner movements not only produce corresponding outer movements: this is the law which operates beneath all physical appearances. He who practices these exercises of bilocation will develop unusual powers of concentration and quiescence and will inevitably achieve waking consciousness on the inner and dimensionally larger world.

Actualizing strongly, she fulfilled her desire, for, viewing the city from the feeling of her wish fulfilled, she matched the state desired and granted that to herself which sleeping men ask of God.

HIGHWAYS OF THE INNER WORLD

To realize your desire, an action must start in your imagination, apart from the evidence of the senses, involving movement of self and implying fulfillment of your desire. Whenever it is the action which the outer self takes to appease desire, that desire will be realized.

The movement of every visible object is caused not by things outside the body, but by things within it, which operate from within outward. The journey is in yourself. You travel along the highways of the inner world. Without inner movement, it is impossible to bring forth anything. Inner action is introverted sensation. If you will construct mentally a drama which implies that you have realized your objective, then close your eyes and drop your thoughts inward, centering your imagination all the while in the predetermined action and partake in that action, you will become a self-determined being.

Inner action orders all things according to the nature of itself. Try it and see whether a desirable ideal once formulated is possible, for only by this process of experiment can you realize your potentialities.

HIGHWAYS OF THE INNER WORLD

It is thus that this creative principle is being realized. So the clue to purposive living is to center your imagination in the action and feeling of fulfilled desire with such awareness, such sensitiveness, that you initiate and experience movement upon the inner world.

Ideas only act if they are felt, if they awaken inner movement. Inner movement is conditioned by self-motivation, outer movement by compulsion.

> Wherever the sole of your foot shall tread,
> the same give I unto you.
> . . . Joshua 1:3

and remember,

> The Lord thy God in the midst of thee is
> mighty.
> . . . Zephaniah 3:17

44

THE PRUNING SHEARS OF REVISION

The second Man is the Lord from Heaven.
. . . 1Corinthians 15:47

Never will he say caterpillars. He'll say,
"There's a lot of butterflies-as-is-to-be on
our cabbages, Prue."He won't say, "It's
winter."He'll say, "Summer's sleeping."And
there's no bud little enough nor sad-colored
enough for Kester not to callen it the
beginnings of the blow.
. . . Mary Webb, Precious Bane

THE VERY first act of correction or cure is always "revise". One must start with oneself. It is one's attitude that must be changed.

What we are, that only can we see.
. . . Emerson

It is a most healthy and productive exercise to daily relive the day as you wish you had lived it, revising the scenes to make them conform to your ideals. For instance, suppose today's mail brought disappointing news. Revise the letter. Mentally rewrite it and make it conform to the news you wish you had received. Then, in imagination, read the revised letter over and over again. This is the essence of revision, and revision results in repeal.

The one requisite is to arouse your attention in a way and to such intensity that you become wholly absorbed in the revised action. You will experience an expansion and refinement of the senses by this imaginative exercise and eventually achieve vision. But always remember that the ultimate purpose of this exercise is to create in you "the Spirit of Jesus", which is continual forgiveness of sin.

Revision is of greatest importance when the motive is to change oneself, when there is a sincere desire to be something different, when the longing is to awaken the ideal active spirit of forgiveness. Without imagination, man remains a being of sin. Man either goes forward to imagination or remains imprisoned in his senses. To go forward to imagination is to forgive. Forgiveness is the life of the imagination. The art of living is the art of forgiving. Forgiveness is, in fact, experiencing in imagination the revised version of the day, experiencing in imagination what you wish you had experienced in the flesh. Every time one really forgives – that is, every time one relives the event as it should have been lived – one is born again.

"Father, forgive them" is not the plea that comes once a year but the opportunity that comes every day. The idea of forgiving is a daily possibility, and, if it is sincerely done, it will lift man to higher and higher levels of being. He will experience a daily Easter, and Easter is the idea of rising transformed. And that should be almost a continuous process.

Freedom and forgiveness are indissolubly linked. Not to forgive is to be at war with ourselves, for we are freed according to our capacity to forgive.

Forgive, and you shall be forgiven.
. . . Luke 6:37

Forgive, not merely from a sense of duty or service; forgive because you want to.

Thy ways are ways of pleasantness and all thy paths are peace.

47

THE PRUNING SHEARS OF REVISION

. . . Proverbs 3:17

You must take pleasure in revision. You can forgive others effectively only when you have a sincere desire to identify them with their ideal. Duty has no momentum. Forgiveness is a matter of deliberately withdrawing attention from the unrevised day and giving it full strength, and joyously, to the revised day. If a man begins to revise even a little of the vexations and troubles of the day, then he begins to work practically on himself. Every revision is a victory over himself and therefore a victory over his enemy.

A man's foes are those
of his own household.
. . . Matthew 10:36

and his household is his state of mind. He changes his future as he revises his day.

When a man practices the art of forgiveness, of revision, however factual the scene on which sight then rests, he revises it with his imagination and gazes on one never before witnessed. The magnitude of the change which any act of revision involves makes such change appear wholly improbable to the realist – the unimaginative man;

but the radical changes in the fortunes of the Prodigal were all produced by a "change of heart".

The battle man fights is fought out in his own imagination. The man who does not revise the day has lost the vision of that life, into the likeness of which it is the true labour of the "Spirit of Jesus" to transform this life.

> All things whatsoever ye would that men
> should do to you, even so do ye to them:
> for this is the law.
> . . . Matthew 7:12

Here is the way an artist friend forgave herself and was set free from pain, annoyance and unfriendliness. Knowing that nothing but forgetfulness and forgiveness will bring us to new values, she cast herself upon her imagination and escaped from the prison of her senses. She writes:

"Thursday, I taught all day in the art school. Only one small thing marred the day. Coming into my afternoon classroom, I discovered the janitor had left all the chairs on top of the desks after cleaning the floor. As I lifted a chair down, it slipped from my grasp and struck me a sharp blow on the instep of my right foot. I immediately

49

examined my thoughts and found that I had criticized the man for not doing his job properly. Since he had lost his helper, I realized he probably felt he had done more than enough and it was an unwanted gift that had bounced and hit me on the foot. Looking down at my foot, I saw both my skin and nylons were intact, so forgot the whole thing.

"That night, after I had been working intensely for about three hours on a drawing, I decided to make myself a cup of coffee. To my utter amazement, I couldn't manage my right foot at all and it was giving out great bumps of pain. I hopped over to a chair and took off my slipper to look at it. The entire foot was a strange purplish pink, swollen out of shape and red hot. I tried walking on it and found that it just flapped. I had no control over it whatsoever. It looked like one of two things: either I had cracked a bone when I dropped the chair on it or something could be dislocated.

"'No use speculating what it is. Better get rid of it right away.' So I became quiet, all ready to melt myself into light. To my complete bewilderment, my imagination refused to cooperate. It just said 'No.' This sort of thing often happens when I am painting. I just started to argue

THE PRUNING SHEARS OF REVISION

'Why not?' It just kept saying 'No.' Finally, I gave up and said, 'You know I am in pain. I am trying hard not to be frightened, but you are the boss. What do you want to do?'

The answer: 'Go to bed and review the day's events.'

So I said 'All right. But let me tell you if my foot isn't perfect by tomorrow morning, you have only yourself to blame.'

"After arranging the bed clothes so they didn't touch my foot, I started to review the day. It was slow going as I had difficulty keeping my attention away from my foot. I went through the whole day, saw nothing to add to the chair incident. But when I reached the early evening, I found myself coming face to face with a man who for the past year has made a point of not speaking. The first time this happened, I thought he had grown deaf. I had known him since school days, but we had never done more than say 'hello' and comment on the weather. Mutual friends assured me I had done nothing, that he had said he never liked me and finally decided it was not worthwhile speaking. I had said 'Hi!'

THE PRUNING SHEARS OF REVISION

He hadn't answered. I found that I thought 'Poor guy – what a horrid state to be in. I shall do something about this ridiculous state of affairs.' So, in my imagination, I stopped right there and re-did the scene. I said 'Hi!' He answered 'Hi!' and smiled. I now thought 'Good old Ex.'s ran the scene over a couple of times and went on to the next incident and finished up the day.

"'Now what – do we do my foot or the concert?' I had been melting and wrapping up a wonderful present of courage and success for a friend who was to make her debut the following day and I had been looking forward to giving it to her tonight. My imagination sounded a little bit solemn as it said 'Let us do the concert. It will be more fun.' But first couldn't we just take my perfectly good imagination foot out of this physical one before we start?' I pleaded. 'By all means.'

"That done, I had a lovely time at the concert and my friend got a tremendous ovation.

"By now I was very, very sleepy and fell asleep doing my project. The next morning, as I was putting on my slipper, I suddenly had a quick memory picture of withdrawing a discolored and swollen foot from the same slipper. I took my foot out and looked at it. It was perfectly normal in every respect. There was a tiny pink spot on the instep where I remembered I had hit it with the chair.' What a vivid dream that was!' I thought and dressed. While waiting for my coffee, I wandered over to my drafting table and saw that all my brushes were lying helter-skelter and unwashed. 'Whatever possessed you to leave your brushes like that?''Don't you remember? It was because of your foot.' So it hadn't been a dream after all, but a beautiful healing."

She had won by the art of revision what she would never have won by force.

> In Heaven, the only Art of Living Is
> Forgetting & Forgiving. Especially to the
> Female.
> . . . Blake

We should take our life, not as it appears to be, but from the vision of this artist, from the vision of the world made perfect that is buried under all minds – buried and waiting for us to revise the day.

> We are led to believe a lie when we see
> with, not through the eye.

THE PRUNING SHEARS OF REVISION

. . . Blake

A revision of the day, and what she held to be so stubbornly real was no longer so to her and, like a dream, had quietly faded away.

You can revise the day to please yourself and by experiencing in imagination the revised speech and actions not only modify the trend of your life story but turn all its discords into harmonies. The one who discovers the secret of revision cannot do otherwise than let himself be guided by love. Your effectiveness will increase with practice. Revision is the way by which right can find its appropriate might.

"Resist not evil", for all passionate conflicts result in an interchange of characteristics.

To him that knoweth to do good, and doeth
it not, to him it is sin.
. . . James 4:17

To know the truth, you must live the truth, and to live the truth, your inner actions must match the actions of your fulfilled desire. Expectancy and desire must become one.

THE PRUNING SHEARS OF REVISION

Your outer world is only actualized inner movement. Through ignorance of the law of revision, those who take to warfare are perpetually defeated.

Only concepts that idealize depict the truth.

Your ideal of man is his truest self. It is because I firmly believe that whatever is most profoundly imaginative is, in reality, most directly practical that I ask you to live imaginatively and to think into, and to personally appropriate the transcendent saying "Christ in you, the hope of glory."

Don't blame; only resolve. It is not man and the earth at their loveliest, but you practicing the art of revision make paradise. The evidence of this truth can lie only in your own experience of it. Try revising the day. It is to the pruning shears of revision that we owe our prime fruit.

THE COIN OF HEAVEN

"Does a firm persuasion that a thing is so,
make it so?" And the prophet replied, "All
poets believe that it does. And in ages of
imagination, this firm persuasion removed
mountains: but many are not capable of a
firm persuasion of anything."
. . . Blake, Marriage of Heaven and Hell

Let every man be fully persuaded
in his own mind.
. . . Romans 14:5

PERSUASION IS an inner effort of intense
attention. To listen attentively as though you heard
is to evoke, to activate. By listening, you can hear
what you want to hear and persuade those beyond
the range of the outer ear. Speak it inwardly in
your imagination only. Make your inner
conversation match your fulfilled desire. What you
desire to hear without, you must hear within.
Embrace the without within and become one who
hears only that which implies the fulfillment of his
desire, and all the external happenings in the world

will become a bridge leading to the objective realization of your desire.

Your inner speech is perpetually written all around you in happenings. Learn to relate these happenings to your inner speech and you will become self-taught. By inner speech is meant those mental conversations which you carry on with yourself. They may be inaudible when you are awake because of the noise and distractions of the outer world of becoming, but they are quite audible in deep meditation and dream. But whether they be audible or inaudible, you are their author and fashion your world in their likeness.

There is a God in heaven [and heaven is within you] that revealeth secrets, and maketh known to the king Nebuchadnezzar what shall be in the latter days. Thy dream, and the visions of thy head upon thy bed, are these.
. . . Daniel 2:28

Inner speech from premises of fulfilled desire is the way to create an intelligible world for yourself.

THE COIN OF HEAVEN

Observe your inner speech for it is the cause of future action. Inner speech reveals the state of consciousness from which you view the world. Make your inner speech match your fulfilled desire, for your inner speech is manifested all around you in happenings.

> If any man offend not in word, the same is a
> perfect man and able also to bridle the whole
> body. Behold, we put bits in the horses'
> mouths, that they may obey us; and we turn
> about their whole body. Behold also the
> ships, which though they be so great, and are
> driven by fierce winds, yet are they turned
> about with a very small helm, whithersoever
> the governor listeth. Even so the tongue is a
> little member, and boasteth great things.
> Behold, how great a matter a little fire
> kindleth!
> . . . James 3:2-5

The whole manifested world goes to show us what use we have made of the Word – Inner Speech. An uncritical observation of our inner talking will reveal to us the ideas from which we view the world. Inner talking mirrors our imagination, and our imagination mirrors the state with which it is fused. If the state with which we are fused is the cause of the phenomenon of our life, then we are relieved of the burden of wondering what to do, for we have no alternative but to identify ourselves with our aim, and inasmuch as the state with which we are identified mirrors itself in our inner speech, then to change the state with which we are fused, we must first change our inner talking. It is our inner conversations which make tomorrow's facts.

> Put off the former conversation, the old
> man, which is corrupt... and be renewed in
> the spirit of your mind... put on the new
> man, which is created in righteousness.
> . . . Ephesians 4:22-24

> Our minds, like our stomachs, are whetted
> by change of food.
> . . . Quintillian

Stop all of the old mechanical negative inner talking and start a new positive and constructive inner speech from premises of fulfilled desire. Inner talking is the beginning, the sowing of the seeds of future action. To determine the action, you must consciously initiate and control your inner talking.

THE COIN OF HEAVEN

Construct a sentence which implies the fulfillment of your aim, such as "I have a large, steady, dependable income, consistent with integrity and mutual benefit", or "I am happily married", "I am wanted", "I am contributing to the good of the world", and repeat such a sentence over and over until you are inwardly affected by it. Our inner speech represents in various ways the world we live in.

In the beginning was the Word.
. . . John 1:1

That which ye sow ye reap. See yonder fields! The sesamum was sesamum, the corn was corn. The Silence and the Darkness knew! So is a man's fate born.
. . . The Light of Asia

Ends run true to origins.

Those that go searching for love only make manifest their own lovelessness. And the loveless never find love, only the loving find love, and they never have to seek for it.
. . . D. H. Lawrence

THE COIN OF HEAVEN

Man attracts what he is. The art of life is to sustain the feeling of the wish fulfilled and let things come to you, not to go after them or think they flee away.

Observe your inner talking and remember your aim. Do they match? Does your inner talking match what you would say audibly had you achieved your goal? The individual's inner speech and actions attract the conditions of his life. Through uncritical self-observation of your inner talking you find where you are in the inner world, and where you are in the inner world is what you are in the outer world. You put on the new man whenever ideals and inner speech match. In this way alone can the new man be born.

Inner talking matures in the dark. From the dark it issues into the light. The right inner speech is the speech that would be yours were you to realize your ideal. In other words, it is the speech of fulfilled desire.

"I am that."

There are two gifts which God has bestowed upon man alone, and on no other mortal creature. These two are mind and speech;

THE COIN OF HEAVEN

and the gift of mind and speech is equivalent
to that of immortality. If a man uses these
two gifts rightly, he will differ in nothing
from the immortals... and when he quits the
body, mind and speech will be his guides,
and by them he will be brought into the
troop of the gods and the souls that have
attained to bliss.
. . . Hermetica, Walter Scott's translation

The circumstances and conditions of life are
out pictured inner talking, solidified sound. Inner
speech calls events into existence. In every event is
the creative sound that is its life and being. All that
a man believes and consents to as true reveals itself
in his inner speech. It is his Word, his life.

Try to notice what you are saying in yourself
at this moment, to what thoughts and feelings you
are consenting. They will be perfectly woven into
your tapestry of life. To change your life, you must
change your inner talking, for "life", said Hermes,
"is the union of Word and Mind". When
imagination matches your inner speech to fulfilled
desire, there will then be a straight path in yourself
from within out, and the without will instantly
reflect the within for you, and you will know
reality is only actualized inner talking.

THE COIN OF HEAVEN

Receive with meekness the inborn Word
which is able to save your souls.
. . . James 1:21

Every stage of man's progress is made by the
conscious exercise of his imagination matching his
inner speech to his fulfilled desire. Because man
does not perfectly match them, the results are
uncertain, while they might be perfectly certain.
Persistent assumption of the wish fulfilled is the
means of fulfilling the intention. As we control our
inner talking, matching it to our fulfilled desires,
we can lay aside all other processes. Then we
simply act by clear imagination and intention. We
imagine the wish fulfilled and carryon mental
conversations from that premise.

Through controlled inner talking from
premises of fulfilled desire, seeming miracles are
performed. The future becomes the present and
reveals itself in our inner speech. To be held by the
inner speech of fulfilled desire is to be safely
anchored in life. Our lives may seem to be broken
by events, but they are never broken so long as we
retain the inner speech of fulfilled desire. All
happiness depends on the active voluntary use of
imagination to construct and inwardly affirm that
we are what we want to be. We match ourselves to

our ideals by constantly remembering our aim and identifying ourselves with it. We fuse with our aims by frequently occupying the feeling of our wish fulfilled. It is the frequency, the habitual occupancy, that is the secret of success. The oftener we do it, the more natural it is. Fancy assembles. Continuous imagination fuses.

It is possible to resolve every situation by the proper use of imagination. Our task is to get the right sentence, the one which implies that our desire is realized, and fire the imagination with it. All this is intimately connected with the mystery of "the still small voice".

Inner talking reveals the activities of imagination, activities which are the causes of the circumstances of life. As a rule, man is totally unaware of his inner talking and therefore sees himself not as the cause but the victim of circumstance. To consciously create circumstance, man must consciously direct his inner speech, matching "the still small voice" to his fulfilled desires.

He calls things not seen as though they were
. . . Romans 4:17

THE COIN OF HEAVEN

Right inner speech is essential. It is the greatest of the arts. It is the way out of limitation into freedom. Ignorance of this art has made the world a battlefield and penitentiary where blood and sweat alone are expected, when it should be a place of marveling and wondering. Right inner talking is the first step to becoming what you want to be.

> Speech is an image of mind,
> and mind is an image of God.
> . . . Hermetica, Scott translation

On the morning of April 12, 1953, my wife was awakened by the sound of a great voice of authority speaking within her and saying, "You must stop spending your thoughts, time, and money. Everything in life must be an investment."

To spend is to waste, to squander, to layout without return. To invest is to layout for a purpose from which a profit is expected. This revelation of my wife is about the importance of the moment. It is about the transformation of the moment. What we desire does not lie in the future but in ourselves at this very moment. At any moment in our lives, we are faced with an infinite choice: "what we are and what we want to be". And what we want to be

THE COIN OF HEAVEN

is already existent, but to realize it we must match our inner speech and actions to it.

> If two of you shall agree on earth as
> touching anything that they shall ask, it shall
> be done for them of My Father
> which is in heaven.
> . . . Matthew 18:19

It is only what is done now that counts. The present moment does not recede into the past. It advances into the future to confront us, spent or invested.

Thought is the coin of heaven. Money is its earthly symbol. Every moment must be invested, and our inner talking reveals whether we are spending or investing. Be more interested in what you are inwardly "saying now" than what you "have said" by choosing wisely what you think and what you feel now.

Any time we feel misunderstood, misused, neglected, suspicious, afraid, we are spending our thoughts and wasting our time. Whenever we assume the feeling of being what we want to be, we are investing. We cannot abandon the moment to negative inner talking and expect to retain

command of life. Before us go the results of all
that seemingly is behind. Not gone is the last
moment – but oncoming.

> My word shall not return unto Me void, but
> it shall accomplish that which I please, and
> it shall prosper in the thing whereto I sent it.
> . . . Isaiah 55:11

The circumstances of life are the muffled
utterances of the inner talking that made them – the
word made visible.

"The Word", said Hermes, "is Son, and the
Mind is Father of the Word. They are not separate
one from the other; for life is the union of Word
and Mind."

> He willed us forth from Himself by the
> Word of Truth.
> . . . James 1:18

> Let us be imitators of God as dear children
> . . . Ephesians 5:1

and use our inner speech wisely to mold an outer
world in harmony with our ideal.

THE COIN OF HEAVEN

The Lord spake by me, and His
Word was in my tongue.
. . . 2Samuel 23:2

The mouth of God is the mind of man. Feed God only the best.

Whatsoever things are of good report...
think on these things.
. . . Philippians 4:8

The present moment is always precisely right for an investment, to inwardly speak the right word.

The word is very near to you, in your mouth,
and in your heart, that you may do it. See, I
have set before you this day life and good,
death and evil, blessings and cursings.
Choose life.
. . . Deuteronomy 30:14, 15, 19

You choose life and good and blessings by being that which you choose. Like is known to like alone. Make your inner speech bless and give good reports. Man's ignorance of the future is the result of his ignorance of his inner talking. His inner talking mirrors his imagination, and his imagination is a government in which the opposition never comes into power.

If the reader ask, "What if the inner speech remains subjective and is unable to find an object for its love?", the answer is: it will not remain subjective, for the very simple reason that inner speech is always objectifying itself. What frustrates and festers and becomes the disease that afflicts humanity is man's ignorance of the art of matching inner words to fulfilled   desire. Inner speech mirrors imagination, and imagination is Christ.

Alter your inner speech, and your perceptual world changes. Whenever inner speech and desire are in conflict, inner speech invariably wins. Because inner speech objectifies itself, it is easy to see that if it matches desire, desire will be objectively realized. Were this not so, I would say with Blake,

Sooner murder an infant in its cradle than nurse unacted desires. But I know from experience,

The tongue... setteth on fire the course of nature.
. . . James 3:6

IT IS WITHIN

. . . Rivers, Mountains, Cities, Villages, All
are Human, & when you enter into
their Bosoms you walk
In Heavens & Earths, as in your own
Bosom you bear your Heaven
And Earth & all you behold; tho' it
appears Without, it is Within,
In your Imagination, of which this World
of Mortality is but a Shadow.
. . . Blake, Jerusalem

THE INNER world was as real to Blake as the outer land of waking life. He looked upon his dreams and visions as the realities of the forms of nature. Blake reduced everything to the bedrock of his own consciousness.

The Kingdom of Heaven is within you.

. . . Luke 17:21

The Real Man, the Imaginative Man, has invested the outer world with all of its properties.

71

IT IS WITHIN

The apparent reality of the outer world which is so hard to dissolve is only proof of the absolute reality of the inner world of his own imagination.

No man can come to me, except the Father
which hath sent me draw him...
I and My Father are One.
. . . John 6:44; 10:30

The world which is described from observation is a manifestation of the mental activity of the observer. When man discovers that his world is his own mental activity made visible, that no man can come unto him except he draws him, and that there is no one to change but himself, his own imaginative self, his first impulse is to reshape the world in the image of his ideal. But his ideal is not so easily incarnated. In that moment when he ceases to conform to external discipline, he must impose upon himself a far more rigorous discipline, the self-discipline upon which the realization of his ideal depends.

Imagination is not entirely untrammeled and free to move at will without any rules to constrain it. In fact, the contrary is true. Imagination travels according to habit. Imagination has choice, but it chooses according to habit. Awake or asleep, man's imagination is constrained to follow certain definite patterns. It is this benumbing influence of habit that man must change; if he does not, his dreams will fade under the paralysis of custom.

Imagination, which is Christ in man, is not subject to the necessity to produce only that which is perfect and good. It exercises its absolute freedom from necessity by endowing the outer physical self with free will to choose to follow good or evil, order or disorder.

Choose this day whom ye will serve.
. . . Joshua 24:15

But after the choice is made and accepted so that it forms the individual's habitual consciousness, then imagination manifests its infinite power and wisdom by molding the outer sensuous world of becoming in the image of the habitual inner speech and actions of the individual.

To realize his ideal, man must first change the pattern which his imagination has followed. Habitual thought is indicative of character. The way to change the outer world is to make the inner speech and action match the outer speech and action of fulfilled desire.

73

IT IS WITHIN

Our ideals are waiting to be incarnated, but unless we ourselves match our inner speech and action to the speech and action of fulfilled desire, they are incapable of birth. Inner speech and action are the channels of God's action. He cannot respond to our prayer unless these paths are offered. The outer behavior of man is mechanical. It is subject to the compulsion applied to it by the behavior of the inner self, and old habits of the inner self hang on till replaced by new ones. It is a peculiar property of the second or inner man that he gives to the outer self, something similar to his own reality of being. Any change in the behavior of the inner self will result in corresponding outer changes.

The mystic calls a change of consciousness "death". By death he means, not the destruction of imagination and the state with which it was fused, but the dissolution of their union. Fusion is union rather than oneness. Thus the conditions to which that union gave being vanish. "I die daily", said Paul to the Corinthians. Blake said to his friend Crabbe Robinson:

> There is nothing like death. Death is the best
> thing that can happen in life; but most
> people die so late and take such an

unmerciful time in dying. God knows, their neighbors never see them rise from the dead.

To the outer man of sense, who knows nothing of the inner man of Being, this is sheer nonsense. But Blake made the above quite clear when he wrote in the year before he died:

William Blake – one who is very much delighted with being in good company. Born 28 November
1757 in London and has died several times since.

When man has the sense of Christ as his imagination, he sees why Christ must die and rise again from the dead to save man – why he must detach his imagination from his present state and match it to a higher concept of himself if he would rise above his present limitations and thereby save himself.

Here is a lovely story of a mystical death which was witnessed by a "neighbor". "Last week", writes the one "who rose from the dead", "a friend offered me her home in the mountains for the Christmas holidays as she thought she might go east. She said that she would let me know this week. We had a very pleasant conversation and I mentioned you and your teaching in connection with a discussion of Dunne's 'Experiment with Time' which she had been reading.

"Her letter arrived Monday. As I picked it up, I had a sudden sense of depression. However, when I read it, she said I could have the house and told me where to get the keys. Instead of being cheerful, I grew still more depressed, so much so I decided there must have been something between the lines which I was getting intuitively. I unfolded the letter and read the first page through and as I turned to the second page, I noticed she had written a postscript on the back of the first sheet. It consisted of an extremely blunt and heavy-handed description of an unlovely trait in my character which I had struggled for years to overcome, and for the past two years I thought I had succeeded. Yet here it was again, described with clinical exactitude.

"I was stunned and desolated. I thought to myself, 'What is this letter trying to tell me? In the first place, she invited me to use her house, as I have been seeing myself in some lovely home during the holidays. In the second place, nothing comes to me except I draw it. And thirdly I have been hearing nothing but good news. So the obvious conclusion is that something in me corresponds to this letter and no matter what it looks like it is good news.'

I reread the letter and as I did so, I asked, 'What is there here for me to see?' And then I saw. It started out, 'After our conversation of last week, I feel I can tell you...' and the rest of the page was as studded with 'weres' and 'wases' as currants in a seed cake. A great feeling of elation swept over me. It was all in the past. The thing I had labored so long to correct was done. I suddenly realized that my friend was a witness to my resurrection. I whirled around the studio, chanting, 'It's all in the past! It is done. Thank you, it is done!'I gathered all my gratitude up in a big ball of light and shot it straight to you and if you saw a flash of lightning Monday evening shortly after six your time, that was it.

"Now, instead of writing a polite letter because it is the correct thing to do, I can write giving sincere thanks for her frankness and thanking her for the loan of her house. Thank you so much for your teaching, which has made my beloved imagination truly my Savior."

IT IS WITHIN

And now, if any man shall say unto her
"Lo, here is Christ, or there",

she will believe it not, for she knows that the
Kingdom of God is within her and that she herself
must assume full responsibility for the incarnation
of her ideal and that nothing but death and
resurrection will bring her to it. She has found her
Savior, her beloved Imagination, forever
expanding in the bosom of God.

There is only one reality, and that is Christ –
Human Imagination, the inheritance and final
achievement of the whole of Humanity,

That we... speaking the truth in love, may
grow up into Him in all things, which is the
head, even Christ.
. . . Ephesians 4:14, 15

CREATION IS FINISHED

I am the beginning and the end, there is
nothing to come that has not been, and is.
. . . Ecclesiastes 3:15 ERV

BLAKE SAW all possible human situations as
"already-made" states. He saw every aspect, every
plot and drama as already worked out as "mere
possibilities" as long as we are not in them, but as
overpowering realities when we are in them. He
described these states as "Sculptures of Los's
Halls".

Distinguish therefore states from Individuals
in those States. States change but Individual
Identities never change nor cease...
The Imagination is not a State.

Said Blake,

It is the Human Existence itself. Affection or
Love becomes a State when divided from
imagination.

CREATION IS FINISHED

Just how important this is to remember is almost impossible to say, but the moment the individual realizes this for the first time is the most momentous in his life, and to be encouraged to feel this is the highest form of encouragement it is possible to give.

This truth is common to all men, but the consciousness of it – and much more, the self-consciousness of it – is another matter.

The day I realized this great truth – that everything in my world is a manifestation of the mental activity which goes on within me, and that the conditions and circumstances of my life only reflect the state of consciousness with which I am fused – is the most momentous in my life.

But the experience that brought me to this certainty is so remote from ordinary existence, I have long hesitated to tell it, for my reason refused to admit the conclusions to which the experience impelled me. Nevertheless, this experience revealed to me that I am supreme within the circle of my own state of consciousness and that it is the state with which I am identified that determines what I experience. Therefore it should be shared with all, for to know this is to become free from the world's greatest tyranny, the belief in a second cause.

> Blessed are the pure in heart:
> for they shall see God.
> . . . Matthew 5:8

Blessed are they whose imagination has been so purged of the beliefs in second causes they know that imagination is all, and all is imagination.

One day I quietly slipped from my apartment in New York City into some remote yesteryear's countryside. As I entered the dining room of a large inn, I became fully conscious. I knew that my physical body was immobilized on my bed back in New York. Yet here I was as awake and as conscious as I have ever been. I intuitively knew that if I could stop the activity of my mind, everything before me would freeze. No sooner was the thought born than the urge to try it possessed me. I felt my head tighten, then thicken to a stillness. My attention concentrated into a crystal-clear focus, and the waitress walking, walked not. And I looked through the window and the leaves falling, fell not. And the family of four eating, ate not. And they lifting the food, lifted it not. Then my attention relaxed, the tightness eased, and of a sudden all moved onward in their course. The leaves fell, the waitress walked and the family ate. Then I understood Blake's vision of the "Sculptures of Los's Halls".

> I sent you to reap that whereon
> ye bestowed no labor.
> . . . John 4:38

Creation is finished.

> I am the beginning and the end, there is
> nothing to come that has not been, and is.
> . . . Ecclesiastes 3:15, ERV

The world of creation is finished and its original is within us. We saw it before we set forth, and have since been trying to remember it and to activate sections of it. There are infinite views of it. Our task is to get the right view and by determined direction of our attention make it pass in procession before the inner eye. If we assemble the right sequence and experience it in imagination until it has the tone of reality, then we consciously create circumstances. This inner procession is the activity of imagination that must be consciously directed. We, by a series of mental transformations, become aware of increasing portions of that which already is, and by matching our own mental activity to that portion of creation which we desire to experience, we activate it, resurrect it, and give it life.

This experience of mine not only shows the world as a manifestation of the mental activity of the individual observer, but it also reveals our course of time as jumps of attention between eternal moments. An infinite abyss separates any two moments of ours. We, by the movements of our attention, give life to the "Sculptures of Los's Halls".

Think of the world as containing an infinite number of states of consciousness from which it could be viewed. Think of these states as rooms or mansions in the House of God, and like the rooms of any house, they are fixed relative to one another. But think of yourself, the Real Self, the Imaginative You, as the living, moving occupant of God's House. Each room contains some of Los's Sculptures, with infinite plots and dramas and situations already worked out but not activated. They are activated as soon as Human Imagination enters and fuses with them. Each represents certain mental and emotional activities. To enter a state, man must consent to the ideas and feelings which it represents. These states represent an infinite number of possible mental transformations which man can experience. To move into another state or mansion necessitates a change of beliefs. All that you could ever desire is already present and only waits to be matched by your beliefs. But it must be matched, for that is the necessary condition by which alone it can be activated and objectified. Matching the beliefs of a state is the seeking that finds, the knocking to which it is opened, the asking that receives. Go in and possess the land.

The moment man matches the beliefs of any state, he fuses with it, and this union results in the activation and projection of its plots, plans, dramas, and situations. It becomes the individual's home from which he views the world. It is his workshop, and, if he is observant, he will see outer reality shaping itself upon the model of his... Imagination.

It is for this purpose of training us in image-making that we were made subject to the limitations of the senses and clothed in bodies of flesh. It is the awakening of the imagination, the returning of His Son, that our Father waits for.

CREATION IS FINISHED

The creature was made subject to vanity not
willingly, but by reason of him who
subjected it.
. . . Romans 8:20

But the victory of the Son, the return of the
prodigal, assures us that the creature shall be
delivered from the bondage of corruption
into the glorious liberty of the Sons
[children] of God.
. . . Romans 8:21

We were subjected to this biological
experience because no one can know of
imagination who has not been subjected to the
vanities and limitations of the flesh, who has not
taken his share of Sonship and gone prodigal, who
has not experimented and tasted this cup of
experience; and confusion will continue until man
awakes and a fundamentally imaginative view of
life has been reestablished and acknowledged as
basic.

I should preach... the unsearchable riches of
Christ and make all men see what is the fellowship
of the mystery, which from the beginning of the
world has been hid in God, Who created all things
by Jesus Christ.

CREATION IS FINISHED

... Ephesians 3:8,9

Bear in mind that Christ in you is your imagination.

As the appearance of our world is determined by the particular state with which we are fused, so may we determine our fate as individuals by fusing our imaginations with ideals we seek to realize. On the distinction between our states of consciousness depends the distinction between the circumstances and conditions of our lives. Man, who is free in his choice of state, often cries out to be saved from the state of his choice.

And ye shall cry out in that day, because of
your king which ye shall have chosen you;
and the Lord will not hear you in that day.
Nevertheless, the people refused to obey the
voice of Samuel; and they said, Nay; but we
will have a king over us.
... 1Samuel 8:18, 19

Choose wisely the state that you will serve. All states are lifeless until imagination fuses with them.

CREATION IS FINISHED

All things when they are admitted are made
manifest by the light: for everything that is
made manifest is light,
. . . Ephesians 5:13

And

Ye are the light of the world,
. . . Matthew 5:14

by which those ideas to which you have
consented are made manifest.

Hold fast to your ideal. Nothing can take it
from you but your imagination. Don't think of your
ideal, think from it. It is only the ideals from which
you think that are ever realized.

Man lives not by bread alone, but by every
word that proceeds out of the mouth of God
. . . Matthew 4:4
and "the mouth of God" is the mind of man.

Become a drinker and an eater of the ideals
you wish to realize. Have a set, definite aim or
your mind will wander, and wandering it eats
every negative suggestion. If you live right
mentally, everything else will be right. By a

change of mental diet, you can alter the course of observed events. But unless there is a change of mental diet, your personal history remains the same. You illuminate or darken your life by the ideas to which you consent. Nothing is more important to you than the ideas on which you feed. And you feed on the ideas from which you think. If you find the world unchanged, it is a sure sign that you are wanting in fidelity to the new mental diet, which you neglect in order to condemn your environment. You are in need of a new and sustained attitude. You can be anything you please if you will make the conception habitual, for any idea which excludes all others from the field of attention discharges in action. The ideas and moods to which you constantly return define the state with which you are fused. Therefore train yourself to occupy more frequently the feeling of your wish fulfilled. This is creative magic. It is the way to work toward fusion with the desired state.

If you would assume the feeling of your wish fulfilled more frequently, you would be master of your fate, but unfortunately you shut out your assumption for all but the occasional hour. Practice making real to yourself the feeling of the wish fulfilled. After you have assumed the feeling of the wish fulfilled, do not close the experience as you would a book, but carry it around like a fragrant odor. Instead of being completely forgotten, let it remain in the atmosphere communicating its influence automatically to your actions and reactions. A mood, often repeated, gains a momentum that is hard to break or check. So be careful of the feelings you entertain. Habitual moods reveal the state with which you are fused.

It is always possible to pass from thinking of the end you desire to realize, to thinking from the end. But the crucial matter is thinking from the end, for thinking from means unification or fusion with the idea: whereas in thinking of the end, there is always subject and object – the thinking individual and the thing thought. You must imagine yourself into the state of your wish fulfilled, in your love for that state, and in so doing, live and think from it and no more of it. You pass from thinking of to thinking from by centering your imagination in the feeling of the wish fulfilled.

THE APPLE OF GOD'S EYE

> What think ye of the Christ?
> Whose Son is He?
> . . . Matthew 22:42

WHEN THIS question is asked of you, let your answer be, "Christ is my imagination", and, though I

> See not yet all things put under him,
> . . . Hebrews 2:8

yet I know that I am Mary from whom sooner or later He shall be born, and eventually

> Do all things through Christ.

The birth of Christ is the awakening of the inner or Second man. It is becoming conscious of the mental activity within oneself, which activity continues whether we are conscious of it or not.

The birth of Christ does not bring any person from a distance, or make anything to be that was not there before. It is the unveiling of the Son of

THE APPLE OF GOD'S EYE

God in man. The Lord "cometh in clouds" is the prophet's description of the pulsating rings of golden liquid light on the head of him in whom He awakes. The coming is from within and not from without, as Christ is in us.

This great mystery

God was manifest in the flesh begins with Advent, and it is appropriate that the cleansing of the Temple,

> Which temple ye are,
> . . . 1Corinthians 3:17

stands in the forefront of the Christian mysteries.

> The Kingdom of Heaven is within you.
> . . . Luke 17:21

Advent is unveiling the mystery of your being. If you will practice the art of revision by a life lived according to the wise, imaginative use of your inner speech and inner actions, in confidence that by the conscious use of "the power that worketh in us" [Ephesians 3:20], Christ will awake in you; if you believe it, trust it, act upon it; Christ will awake in you. This is Advent.

THE APPLE OF GOD'S EYE

Great is the mystery,
God was manifest in the flesh.
. . . 1Timothy 3:16

From Advent on,

He that toucheth you toucheth
the apple of God's eye.
. . . Zechariah 2:8

THE SEARCH

To Victoria

The fulfillment of a dream

ONCE IN an idle interval at sea, I meditated on "the perfect state", and wondered what I would be, were I of too pure eyes to behold iniquity, if to me all things were pure and were I without condemnation. As I became lost in this fiery brooding, I found myself lifted above the dark environment of the senses. So intense was the feeling, I felt myself a being of fire dwelling in a body of air. Voices as from a heavenly chorus, with the exaltation of those who had been conquerors in a conflict with death, were singing "He is risen – He is risen", and intuitively I knew they meant me.

Then I seemed to be walking in the night. I soon came upon a scene that might have been the ancient Pool of Bethesda, for in this place lay a great multitude of impotent folk – blind, halt, withered – waiting not for the moving of the water as of tradition, but waiting for me. As I came near, without thought or effort on my part they were, one after the other, molded as by the Magician of the Beautiful. Eyes, hands, feet – all missing members – were drawn from some invisible reservoir and molded in harmony with that perfection which I felt springing within me. When all were made perfect, the chorus exulted, "It is finished". Then the scene dissolved and I awoke.

I know this vision was the result of my intense meditation upon the idea of perfection, for my meditations invariably bring about union with the state contemplated. I had been so completely absorbed within the idea that for a while I had become what I contemplated, and the high purpose with which I had for that moment identified myself drew the companionship of high things and fashioned the vision in harmony with my inner nature. The ideal with which we are united works by association of ideas to awaken a thousand moods to create a drama in keeping with the central idea.

I first discovered this close relationship of moods to vision when I was aged about seven. I became aware of a mysterious life quickening within me like a stormy ocean of frightening might. I always knew when I would be united with this hidden identity, for my senses were expectant on the nights of these visitations and I knew beyond all doubt that before morning I would be alone with immensity. I so dreaded these visitations that I would lie awake until my eyes from sheer exhaustion closed. As my eyes closed in sleep, I was no longer solitary but smitten through and through with another being, and yet I knew it to be myself. It seemed older than life, yet nearer to me than my boyhood. If I tell what I discovered on these nights, I do so not to impose my ideas on others but that I may give hope to those who seek the law of life.

I discovered that my expectant mood worked as a magnet to unite me with this Greater Me, while my fears made It appear as a stormy sea. As a boy, I conceived of this mysterious self as might, and in my union with It I felt its majesty as a stormy sea which drenched me, then rolled and tossed me as a helpless wave.

As a man I conceived of It as love and myself the son of It, and in my union with It, now, what a love enfolds me! It is a mirror to all. Whatever we conceive It as being, that It is to us. I believe It to be the center through which all the threads of the universe are drawn; therefore I have altered my values and changed my ideas so that they now depend upon and are in harmony with this sole cause of all that is. It is to me that changeless reality which fashions circumstances in harmony with our concepts of ourselves.

My mystical experiences have convinced me that there is no way to bring about the outer perfection we seek other than by the transformation of ourselves.

As soon as we succeed in transforming ourselves, the world will melt magically before our eyes and reshape itself in harmony with that which our transformation affirms.

Two other visions I will tell because they bear out the truth of my assertion that we, by intensity of love and hate, become what we contemplate.

Once, with closed eyes made radiant from brooding, I meditated on the eternal question, "Who Am I?" and felt myself gradually dissolve into a shoreless sea of vibrant light, imagination passing beyond all fear of death. In this state nothing existed but myself, a boundless ocean of liquid light. Never have I felt more intimate with Being.

How long this experience lasted I do not know, but my return to earth was accompanied by a distinct feeling of crystallizing again into human shape.

At another time, I lay on my bed and with my eyes shut as in sleep I brooded on the mystery of Buddha. In a little while, the dark caverns of my brain began to grow luminous.

I seemed to be surrounded by luminous clouds which emanated from my head as fiery, pulsating rings. I saw nothing but these luminous rings for a time. Then there appeared before my eyes a rock of quartz crystal.

While I gazed upon it, the crystal broke into pieces which invisible hands quickly shaped into the living Buddha. As I looked on this meditative figure, I saw that it was myself. I was the living Buddha whom I contemplated. A light like the sun glowed from this living image of myself with increasing intensity until it exploded. Then the light gradually faded and once more I was back within the blackness of my room.

THE SEARCH

Out of what sphere or treasury of design came this being mightier than human, his garments, the crystal, the light? If I saw, heard and moved in a world of real beings when I seemed to myself to be walking in the night, when the lame, the halt, the blind were transformed in harmony with my inner nature, then I am justified in assuming that I have a more subtile body than the physical, a body that can be detached from the physical and used in other spheres; for to see, to hear, to move are functions of an organism however ethereal. If I brood over the alternative that my psychic experiences were self-begotten fantasy, no less am I moved to wonder at this mightier self who flashes on my mind a drama as real as those I experience when I am fully awake.

On these fiery meditations I have entered again and again, and I know beyond all doubt that both assumptions are true. Housed within this form of earth is a body attuned to a world of light, and I have, by intense meditation, lifted it as with a magnet through the skull of this dark house of flesh.

The first time I awoke the fires within me I thought my head would explode. There was intense vibration at the base of my skull, then sudden oblivion of all. Then I found myself clothed in a garment of light and attached by a silvery elastic cord to the slumbering body on the bed. So exalted were my feelings, I felt related to the stars. In this garment I roamed spheres more familiar than earth, but found that, as on earth, conditions were molded in harmony with my nature. "Self-begotten fantasy", I hear you say. No more so than the things of earth.

I am an immortal being conceiving myself as man and forming worlds in the likeness and image of my concept of self.

What we imagine, that we are. By our imagination, we have created this dream of life, and by our imagination we will re-enter that eternal world of light, becoming that which we were before we imagined the world. In the divine economy nothing is lost. We cannot lose anything save by descent from the sphere where the thing has its natural life.

There is no transforming power in death and, whether we are here or there, we fashion the world that surrounds us by the intensity of our imagination and feeling, and we illuminate or darken our lives by the concepts we hold of ourselves. Nothing is more important to us than our conception of ourselves, and especially is this true of our concept of the deep, hidden One within us.

Those that help or hinder us, whether they know it or not, are the servants of that law which shapes outward circumstances in harmony with our inner nature. It is our conception of ourselves which frees or constrains us, though it may use material agencies to achieve its purpose.

Because life molds the outer world to reflect the inner arrangement of our minds, there is no way of bringing about the outer perfection we seek other than by the transformation of ourselves. No help cometh from without; the hills to which we lift our eyes are those of an inner range. It is thus to our own consciousness that we must turn as to the only reality, the only foundation on which all phenomena can be explained. We can rely absolutely on the justice of this law to give us only that which is of the nature of ourselves.

To attempt to change the world before we change our concept of ourselves is to struggle against the nature of things. There can be no outer change until there is first an inner change. As within, so without. I am not advocating philosophical indifference when I suggest that we should imagine ourselves as already that which we want to be, living in a mental atmosphere of greatness, rather than using physical means and arguments to bring about the desired change. Everything we do, unaccompanied by a change of consciousness, is but futile readjustment of surfaces. However we toil or struggle, we can receive no more than our subconscious assumptions affirm.

To protest against anything which happens to us is to protest against the law of our being and our rulership over our own destiny.

The circumstances of my life are too closely related to my conception of myself not to have been launched by my own spirit from some magical storehouse of my being. If there is pain to me in these happenings, I should rook within myself for the cause, for I am moved here and there and made to live in a world in harmony with my concept of myself.

Intense meditation brings about a union with the state contemplated, and during this union we see visions, have experiences, and behave in keeping with our change of consciousness. This shows us that a transformation of consciousness will result in a change of environment and behavior. However, our ordinary alterations of consciousness, as we pass from one state to another, are not transformations, because each of them is so rapidly succeeded by another in the reverse direction; but whenever one state grows so stable as to definitely expel its rivals, then that central habitual state defines the character and is a true transformation. To say that we are transformed means that ideas previously peripheral in our consciousness now take a central place and form the habitual center of our energy.

All wars prove that violent emotions are extremely potent in precipitating mental rearrangements. Every great conflict has been followed by an era of materialism and greed in which the ideals for which the conflict ostensibly was waged are submerged. This is inevitable because war evokes hate, which impels a descent in consciousness from the plane of the ideal to the level where the conflict is waged. If we would become as emotionally aroused over our ideals as we become over our dislikes, we would ascend to the plane of our ideals as easily as we now descend to the level of our hates.

Love and hate have a magical transforming power, and we grow through their exercise into the likeness of what we contemplate. By intensity of hatred we create in ourselves the character we imagine in our enemies. Qualities die for want of attention, so the unlovely states might best be rubbed out by imagining "beauty for ashes and joy for mourning" [Isaiah 61:3] rather than by direct attacks on the state from which we would be free.

"Whatsoever things are lovely and of good report, think on these things" [Philippians 4:8], for we become that with which we are en rapport.

There is nothing to change but our concept of self. Humanity is a single being in spite of its many forms and faces, and there is in it only such seeming separation as we find in our own being when we are dreaming. The pictures and circumstances we see in dreams are creations of our own imagination and have no existence save in ourselves. The same is true of the pictures and circumstances we see in this dream of life. They reveal our concepts of ourselves. As soon as we succeed in transforming self, our world will dissolve and reshape itself in harmony with that which our change affirms.

The universe which we study with such care is a dream, and we the dreamers of the dream, eternal dreamers dreaming non-eternal dreams. One day, like Nebuchadnezzar, we shall awaken from the dream, from the nightmare in which we fought with demons, to find that we really never left our eternal home; that we were never born and have never died save in our dream.

The End

Additional Metaphysical Resources

http://pistissophiaaudio.com/
http://theiamdiscourses.com/
http://asearchforgod.org/
http://iammeditations.org/
http://christreturns.org/
http://jeshuathepersonalchrist.org/

Neville Goddard Books Online

http://www.feelingisthesecret.org/
http://www.atyoucommand.org/
http://www.awakenedimaginationandthesearch.org/
http://www.nevillegoddardfreedomforall.org/
http://www.nevillegoddardoutofthisworld.org/
http://www.prayertheartofbelieving.com/
http://www.nevillegoddardseedtimeandharvest.org/
http://www.thelawandthepromise.com/
http://www.thepowerofawareness.org/
http://www.yourfaithisyourfortune.com/

www.TheSickle.Org
www.TheSharpSickle.Com

www.MetaphysicalPocketBooks.Com
www.Audioenlightenment.Com

www.ingramcontent.com/pod-product-compliance
Lightning Source LLC
Chambersburg PA
CBHW070523030426
42337CB00016B/2077